All O'er t'Parish

A SECOND STROLL AROUND CLIVIGER

TEXT
Peter I. Pomeroy

with the help of the
URBAN STUDIES GROUP
of
Burnley Teachers' Centre

Edwin Ashworth, B.A.   Roger Frost, B.A.
Noel Coates, B.A.   Stuart Gibson, N.D.D., A.T.C.

ARTWORK
Peter Collins, Stewart Gibson, Peter I. Pomeroy, Norman Ward

*   *   *

Lancashire County Council
Library and Leisure Committee
1983

The Ram Inn, 1905. The house next to the Inn was the original vicarage of St. John's Church.

Datestone at the rear of the Ram Inn.

PREFACE

This is the fourth booklet in the series produced by the Urban Studies Group of Burnley Teachers' Centre, a group comprised of members who reflect varying fields of education.

The Group's first publication was the successful "Along t' Cut", a towpath walk along the stretch of the Leeds and Liverpool Canal which passes through Burnley. This was followed by "Top o' th' Town", a guide to the area, centred around St. Peter's Church, formerly occupied by the original village of Burnley. The third booklet was "All O'er t' Parish", a stroll around the north-western part of the Cliviger Valley.

"All O'er t' Parish" was originally envisaged as a single booklet covering two or three short walks in different parts of the district. The wealth of information and photographic material uncovered in the course of researching the walks soon made that idea impractical.

This second stroll in Cliviger follows a trail, commencing and finishing at Holme Chapel, which explores the south-eastern half of the district. It is intended primarily for the walker with an eye for his surroundings. There are fine views to be enjoyed and interesting sites to discover. Careful observation reveals traces of past industries, including pottery sherds at Pot Oven Farm, lead ore fragments on the slopes of Dean Scout and mine spoil containing fossils from the old pit in Black Clough.

Whether you don boots and rucksack or merely browse in a comfortable chair by a cosy fire, we hope that "All O'er t' Parish" will provide an informative guide to a beautiful corner of East Lancashire.

Mounting block, Ram Inn.

3

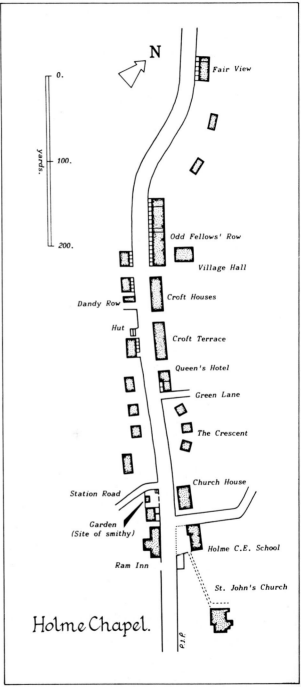

N

Fair View

0.

100.

yards.

200.

Odd Fellows' Row

Village Hall

Dandy Row

Croft Houses

Hut

Croft Terrace

Queen's Hotel

Green Lane

The Crescent

Church House

Station Road

Garden
(Site of smithy)

Holme C.E. School

Ram Inn

St. John's Church

Holme Chapel.

4

Our second walk in Cliviger commences in the village of Holme Chapel. The word 'holme' is Norse in origin and was usually applied to an area of marshy riverside land. Further examples occur along the Calder — Honey Holme, Towneley Holmes and Stoneyholme.

The first walk passed through Walk Mill which had, at various times, a thriving weaving shed, two coal mines, a brewery, an iceworks and an egg-packing station. In contrast, Holme Chapel has retained a more rural character.

Land in Cliviger was administered from Kirkstall Abbey in the twelfth and thirteenth centuries. Part of this land became the estate of the Whitaker family from 1431, possibly even earlier. For some 350 years Cliviger consisted of scattered farms with The Holme, its estate buildings and a chantry chapel at the centre. In 1759 an Act of Parliament authorised the construction of a toll road between Burnley and Todmorden. Thirty years later a new church replaced the dilapidated chapel and around 1800 the first of the terraced houses appeared as the village began to grow. Later rows, built alongside the road, provide a typical example of linear development.

The starting point of the walk is at the Burnley end of Holme Chapel. Here, some 550 yards before the Ram Inn, is an attractive row of cottages. Fair View Buildings consisted of four dwellings when built in the mid-nineteenth century. By the time of the 1861 Census a fifth cottage, in the form of a lean-to extension, had been added at one end of the row. The male occupants of the houses listed in the Census were, with one exception, employed as coalminers. The fifth man was a quarry worker. In the middle of the row a carved stone bears the initials F.V.B., together with the date 1856. Set into the cement rendering of a chimney stack, on the lean-to extension, there appears to be a small stone face.

From Fair View we make our way in the direction of Todmorden. About 150 yards along the road we come to a row of sixteen houses on the left hand side. The style of the houses indicates that the terrace was built in phases.

The first half of the row consists of houses with bay windows. The remaining eight houses at the far end were built first. At a later date five bay fronted houses were erected and a gap was left between the two terraces. The two houses at the Burnley end of the row were added next. The bays of these houses have beautiful stained glass windows depicting birds of prey.

Fair View.

Croft Houses. The side door and the blocked up window suggests that the end houses were originally back to back dwellings.

Dandy Row.

The eight original houses, without bay windows, are known as "Th' Odd Fellows' Row". In the centre of this half of the block is a stone carved with an inscription which gives a clue to the name.

A mistake appears to have been made in the carving of the inscription as the initials should read G.U.O.O.F. The Grand United Order of Odd Fellows. The Odd Fellows are a friendly society whose members are pledged to help one another. Houses such as these were built by the society as a form of investment. Members bought the houses at a slightly lower interest rate than that being charged by the building societies.

The eight houses were built by the Ark of Friendship Lodge 1033, which was the Cliviger branch of the Society. A ninth house was eventually erected by the Society. This filled the gap between the two terraces and was built with a bay window to match the later houses.

For many years the Ark of Friendship Lodge meetings were held at the Ram Inn. Later, meetings took place across the road at St. John's School.

At one time there were as many as nine lodges in the Burnley district but due to closures and amalgamations only two now remain. The oldest of these is the Morning Star Lodge. The other survivor is the Holme Lodge 22, the meetings of which are held at the Junction Hotel, Rosegrove. Previously, this lodge had no connection with Holme Chapel and probably took its name from Holme Lodge. This building stands at the junction of Accrington Road and Rossendale Road and is now the home of Rosegrove Unity Working Men's Club. A former resident at Holme Lodge was Richard Shaw, a solicitor, who was elected as the first Member of Parliament for Burnley in 1868.

The Ark of Friendship Lodge, faced with difficulties in appointing officials, was amalgamated with Holme Lodge 22 in January 1978.

At the end of the row of houses, situated to the rear, is the Village Hall. This red brick structure was erected in 1904 as the Victoria Institute. It was built for prayer meetings and Bible readings by a breakaway group, following a dispute amongst the congregation at St. John's Church. The hall was later presented to the parish when it became impossible to meet the cost of the rate demand.

We resume our walk in the direction of the Ram Inn. Crossing the road at the end of the second row of houses on the right hand side, we come to a pair of cottages which are set end on to the pavement. These buildings, which are known as Dandy Hole, were formerly hand Loom weavers' cottages. The dandy loom was an early nineteenth century development of the handloom, a metal frame version which was more efficient than its wooden predecessor.

Until the middle of the eighteenth century, the textile industry in the Burnley area relied on readily available supplies of local wool. Hand loom weavers worked in their own houses producing woollens and worsteds. In 1750 the weavers of Cliviger produced 3,597 worsted pieces.

The second half the century saw important changes. In Lancashire cotton replaced wool as the basic raw material and the factory system started to develop. The majority of the early mills were concerned with spinning. Although some of the mills contained a small number of hand looms in a separate room, most weavers continued to work at home. Estimated figures for 1831 indicate that domestic weavers out-numbered factory workers by three to one. In the 1851 census, out of 49 weavers in Cliviger, 6 were listed as hand loom weavers. The actual number may have been higher as only 17 were entered as power loom weavers.

At the corner of Dandy Hole, next to the pavement, there is a walled up doorway. This was the beam door. Originally a flight of steps stood here to allow the carrying of cloth beams in and out of the upstairs weaving room.

Another example of a beam door occurs directly across the road in the wall of the row called Croft Houses. This name was probably derived from a nearby patch of land which was formerly an arable enclosure adjoining a dwelling. The houses, which appear to have been built in pairs at different stages, form the oldest terrace in the village, the shot-stone walls being characteristic of housing erected in the period 1790-1810. At the Ram Inn end of the block, the houses were originally back-to-back with three rooms to each.

Farther along, on the right, stands a wooden hut. It was formerly a fish and chip shop and was later converted to a transport cafe. Problems caused by the parking of heavy vehicles led to the closure of the business. In recent years the building has been used as a private workshop.

The row of houses on the left hand side of the road, as we approach the Queen's Hotel, is Croft Terrace. In the middle of the row there is a carved datestone.

Remaining on the same side of the road, we proceed to the Queen's Hotel. High up on the gable end of the building there is a carved plaque.

The letters C.H.B. are likely to stand for Croft House Buildings. It is possible that the initials F.S. are those of Fielding Schofield who, according to the 1861 Census, was a grocer and beer-seller at nearby Hob Lane End. In 1868 "mine hosts" at the Queen's Hotel were Ann and William Schofield. The houses of Croft Terrace were at one time owned by the Schofield family.

Attached to the hotel are two picturesque cottages, the second of which has a verandah with interesting wooden supports. From their appearance these look to be former barn timbers. The end cottage, which is understood to have been an ostler's house at one time, is probably the Hob Lane End where Fielding Schofield carried on his grocery business.

In more recent times Harold Hoyle, a miner at Copy Pit, produced delicious home-made ice-cream here. He used ice produced locally at the Park Road works and milk from the Ram Farm, next to the inn. Before the last war his handcart was a familiar sight at village garden parties and sports days. Wartime rationing meant that the icecream making had to cease for some years. Later he resumed his activities for a short spell, which lasted until the end of the forties.

The semi-detached houses immediately across the road from here have their respective doorways adorned by interesting carved heads.

We continue along the road towards the Ram Inn. On the left-hand side is The Crescent, an attractive development consisting of three pairs of semi-detached houses. Set into the wall alongside the pavement is a datestone.

A former beam door, Croft Houses.

As we approach the Ram Inn, to which we shall return at the end of our walk, the next building on the left of the road is Church House, which was built in 1926. Across the lane on the left, set back from the road, is Holme Church of England Primary School which dates from the first half of the last century. Before the school came into existence the village was served by a "dame school". This type of school, usually run by a spinster or widow, was once common throughout the country. The dame taught very elementary principles of reading and writing, together with knitting and sewing.

Sir James Phillips Kay Shuttleworth of Gawthorpe took a great interest in education and was dissatisfied with the existing provisions. In 1825 he petitioned Parliament for a better system of elementary education for the children of the poorer classes. Eight years later Parliament granted £20,000 for the building of schools. The grant was raised to £30,000 in 1839. These new schools were known as National Schools.

The grant towards a school at Holme fell short of the required amount so Thomas Hordern Whitaker and a body of Trustees raised the extra money. The middle part of the present building is original and was built in the 1830s. The building had an "internal porch" and could be divided into two rooms by a sliding partition.

The first schoolmaster was the Incumbent of St. John's Church, the Rev. John Langfield. He taught at the school until he was replaced by Daniel Langfield of Habergham, after the Crimean War. A greatly loved schoolmaster was Robert Spencer who was appointed in 1875.

In 1890 the school lacked sufficient accommodation. The necessary alterations were undertaken and involved the addition of an extra classroom together with the removal of the internal porch. The school log records the re-opening of the school on 6th January 1890 in the charge of newly appointed schoolmaster, Mr. Harry Buckley. As the alterations to the school building were not quite complete, lessons took place in the long room at The Ram until 10th February. Due to the limited space at the inn the older children had to attend the Mereclough or Walk Mill schools. Further alterations, implemented shortly after World War I, resulted in the building as it exists today.

To the right of the school building is the lychgate of St. John's Church. In Middle English the word for body was *lich* and a lychgate is literally a *corpse* gate, a roofed entrance to a churchyard where the funeral bier rested before the interment. Carved on a beam inside the roof is an inscription to Mary Charlotte Master-Whitaker. The gate was erected as a memorial to his wife by the Rev. Alfred Master-Whitaker, Vicar of the Parish from 1896 until 1916.

After the conquest in 1066, William I apportioned large areas of the country to his loyal supporters. Cliviger, situated in the Honor of Clitheroe, constituted a part of the land "between Ribble and Mersey" which was granted to Roger de Poitou, a cousin of William. For the next three hundred years the Honor of Clitheroe was under the control of powerful barons. During this period occasional changes were made according to the whims of the barons. Two changes of particular interest took place in the twelfth century.

A charter of 1122 granted lands in Burnley to Pontefract Priory. In later years there was considerable disagreement between the Vicars of Whalley and the Priors, concerning their respective rights and title to these lands. The Priory eventually lost control at some time in the ten year period leading up to 1170.

About 1159 lands 'situate at Clivachir' were granted to the Abbot of Kirkstall by Ralph d'Eland. That the Abbots retained control of their lands in Cliviger for over a century is shown by a grant of 1269 in which the Abbot made land east of the Calder available to Matthew, son of Henry de Dyneley.

From this date on there is no further mention of Kirkstall in the affairs of Cliviger, and it would seem that the Abbots had little interest in this part of their estate.

In 1283 a significant change took place in the religious life of the local district. The Parish of Whalley and its dependent chapels, including Burnley, was granted to the monks of Stanlawe Abbey by Henry de Lacy. A few years later the Cistercian monks moved from the Wirral and settled at Whalley. Grants from the de Lacy family, together with tithes collected from the surrounding communities, enriched the new abbey.

This era in the life of the church came to an end in 1536. Henry VIII, coveting the wealth of the church, initiated the Dissolution of the Monasteries.

A chantry chapel in Cliviger was built 'at some date not long before the year 1533' by Richard Whitaker and endowed with three houses and six acres of land. The building was situated at the lower end of the present churchyard. It was constructed of blocks of stone so large that a mere six courses of stonework extended from the foundation to the roof. A single bell was accommodated in a 'bell cote' on the west gable and a cross stood on the opposite end of the roof. The chapel was entered through a small porchway on the south side. Sycamore trees grew around the sides and at the back of the building. A colony of rooks was resident in the trees and in the words of Dr. T. D. Whitaker 'when there was any competition of voices at all, cawing drowned the parson's saw'.

The interior of the building measured 42 feet by 18 feet. The "quire" was described as being decorated with Gothic carved work and inscriptions. These were unfortunately destroyed in 1788, when they might have provided evidence of both the founder and the date of the foundation.

The first recorded priest was Hugh Watmough. About the year 1533 he was appointed at a stipend of £1. 10s. 4d per annum which was drawn from the endowments of Richard Whitaker.

The chantry was suppressed, together with others throughout the country, in 1548. The building remained and was considered to be the property of the Whitaker family. Hugh Watmough probably had his services retained privately by the family and continued to receive the stipend until about 1560.

No further mention of the chapel appears in the records until 1650. At this time, under Cromwellian rule, judicial enquiries were held to seek out vacant chapels where Puritan ministers could be appointed. It was intended that pastorates would be established to encourage eradication of the Anglican and Roman Catholic traditions. An enquiry held at Blackburn noted that the chapel was without a minister or maintenance for its upkeep. The following year Thomas White was appointed to the chapel. His length of sojourn is not recorded. From 1660, the year of the Restoration of the Monarchy, there is no mention of either the chapel or a priest until 1742. In that year Thomas Whitaker nominated Anthony Weatherhead, who was subsequently appointed resident curate. The registers of the church are almost complete from this period onwards.

As a result of the long periods of neglect, the building had fallen into a dilapidated state and was 'growing ruinous'. In 1788 the old chapel was dismantled and the present church was erected on higher ground. Dr. T.D. Whitaker was instrumental in the rebuilding and the cost of £870 was defrayed by the Whitaker family.

Little remains of the chantry building. Part of the stone steps, which led to the chapel, can be seen in the lower course of the churchyard wall alongside the main road.

The new building, then in the Diocese of Chester, was consecrated by the Bishop, Dr. William Cleaver, on 29th July 1794, and is dedicated to St. John the Evangelist. It is constructed in plain Doric style and is surmounted at the west end by an octagonal cupola mounted on a square base. The cupola originally housed a single bell, but in 1895 this was replaced by a peal of eleven bells. The bells were cast at the Whitechapel Bell Foundry of Mears and Stainbank and the cost of £260 was met by Mrs. M.C. Master-Whitaker.

St. John's Church prior to the alterations of 1897.

When first completed, the interior roof was underdrawn and the building contained a three-decker pulpit and sounding board. In 1897 an extension to the church allowed space for a new chancel and the installation of the organ. The chancel and the organ were another gift from Mrs. Master-Whitaker. At the same time the underdrawn roof and the dilapidated three-decker pulpit were removed. The latter was replaced by the present pulpit which is understood to have been purchased from a Leeds workshop and may have been salvaged originally from Kirkstall Abbey. If this were true, the pulpit would provide an interesting link with the past.

The three decker pulpit and sounding board.

The Whitaker Chapel, St. John's Church.

The pulpit, St. John's Church.

The east window was repositioned when the chancel was added and is dated 1850. It was installed in memory of Maria Whitaker. The remaining stained glass windows were, with one exception, erected as memorials to members of the Whitaker family.

On the south side of the nave stands the private chapel of the Whitaker family. Two old pews, one containing miserere stalls, are to be seen in the chapel. The pews were brought from Blackburn Parish Church by Dr. T.D. Whitaker. From the age and style of the pews it would appear that they were originally associated with an abbey or monastery, possibly Whalley Abbey. The chapel contains a bust of Dr. Whitaker and a plain tablet commemorating William and Lucy, the parents of the distinguished historian. Other plaques in the chapel are inscribed to Mary Charlotte Whitaker, who died in 1816 aged 23, and the Rev. Thomas Thoresby Whitaker. The minister was fatally injured on falling from a horse in 1817. The three tablets are inscribed in Latin. Beneath the chapel is the Whitaker family vault. Dr. T.D. Whitaker was interred here in a coffin hollowed out of one of the larch trees of his own planting.

The private chapel of the Ormerod family is on the north side of the nave. On the wall is a monument with the arms of Ormerod impaling those of Legh of Lyme. It commemorates Lawrence Ormerod (1753-1793) and was erected at the request of his widow, Martha Ann, whose own memorial can also be seen. A third tablet is inscribed to their son-in-law John Hargreaves J.P. who served as High Sheriff of Lancashire in 1825. He was a Lieutenant Colonel in command of the 3rd Regiment of the Lancashire Militia. In 1819, a few days after the Peterloo Massacre, the colonel prevented a possible riot at a Radical meeting held in Burnley. The chapel also contains a small painting of General Scarlett and the Roll of Honour from The Great War.

The alabaster font stands next to the pulpit. It is a memorial to the Rev. Daniel Sutcliffe who served the Parish for 36 years (1860-1896). The previous font was associated with the chantry chapel and was removed to The Holme. It served as a bird bath until it was recently stolen from its position in front of the hall. The ewer (water carrier) was a gift of Lady Thursby of Ormerod House.

At the west end of the church is the gallery. Before the building of the new chancel the choir sat here.

Outside the main door, on the south side of the building, there is a small gateway. Above the gate stands the head of an ancient cross which is reputed to have been brought from Whalley Abbey by Dr. Whitaker. On the face of the stone there is a carved representation of a heart with five wounds, affixed to a cross.

The churchyard contains many interesting gravestones. Close to the church, by a higher pathway, is the grave of General Sir James Yorke Scarlett.

On 25th October 1854, the day of the heroic but futile Light Brigade charge against the Russian guns in "the valley of death", General Scarlett earlier led a charge of the Heavy Brigade, which succeeded in halting a much greater force of enemy cavalry. Thirteen years later a pair of captured Russian cannon were presented to the town by the Secretary of State for War. These were positioned at junction of Colne Road and Bank Parade, close the Scarlett's home at Bank Hall. Although the plaque can be seen at the corner which is still referred to as "the Cannons", the guns were taken for scrap during the Second World War.

General Scarlett

General Scarlett's grave.

In 1868 Scarlett stood as the Conservative candidate for Burnley at the first parliamentary election. The Liberal, Richard Shaw, was elected, his 2,620 votes giving him a majority of 382.

The General died in 1871 and it has been estimated that 60,000 people lined the funeral route of this highly respected man, quite remarkable considering that the population of Burnley at the time was about 40,000! Some of his personal effects, including a presentation sword which was paid for by public subscription, are exhibited at Towneley Hall.

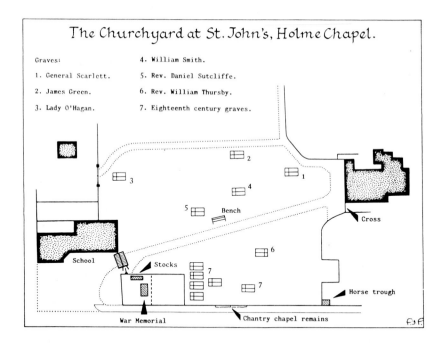

The Churchyard at St. John's, Holme Chapel.

Graves:

1. General Scarlett.
2. James Green.
3. Lady O'Hagan.
4. William Smith.
5. Rev. Daniel Sutcliffe.
6. Rev. William Thursby.
7. Eighteenth century graves.

School

Stocks

Bench

Cross

Horse trough

War Memorial

Chantry chapel remains

A short distance along the higher pathway, on the left, a small stone cross marks the grave of James Green of The Haven, Portsmouth. In addition to being a colliery owner employing 170 men and a cotton spinner with 60 employees (1851 Census), Mr. Green was the architect of several notable buildings. He studied architecture with Leigh Hall of Bolton and civil engineering under the famous George Stephenson and T.L. Gooch. The latter was the surveyor of the Todmorden-Burnley railway line, opened by the Lancashire and Yorkshire Railway Company in 1849.

Aenon Chapel, St. Stephen's Church and the Mechanics Institute provide examples of Mr. Green's work in Burnley. One of his major achievements was the old Burnley Market Hall. A reproduction of his drawing for this building was presented to Towneley Hall by his daughters in 1831.

Mr. Green was the architect of Accrington Town Hall. Built as the Peel Institute in 1857-58, it commemorated the Peel Family, the largest employers in the district. New Jerusalem Church, Accrington, St. Luke's Church, Brierfield, Cornholme Methodist Chapel and School, Portsmouth Mill and Stoodley Pike bear further testimony to his planning.

At the far end of the churchyard, directly opposite the church door, a carved stone cross marks the grave of Lady O'Hagan. Alice Mary

16

Towneley, the first Baroness O'Hagan, was the third daughter of Colonel Charles Towneley. Her activities and interests were many. She supported all forms of social work and was a great educational worker, serving on the Burnley School Board, and later, as a member of Burnley Education Committee.

Midway between the two paths, in line with the grave of James Green, is the tomb of William Smith, who was an earthenware manufacturer at the Long Causeway pottery.

About halfway down the lower pathway, on the top side close to a bench, lies the grave of the Rev. Daniel Sutcliffe.

On the lower side of the path, slightly nearer to the church, a white marble grave faces west. Here, the Rev. William Thursby was buried, in the tradition of the clergy facing his parishioners. He lived at Ormerod Hall and served the parish for 34 years. In 1869 the health of his wife, Eleanor Mary, caused the family to move to Brighton.

The Thursby Family were great supporters of the Church. William, together with his brother-in-law, General Scarlett, presented land for St. Paul's Church, Saunder Bank. He made a considerable contribution when St. Luke's Church, Brierfield was built and he provided £8,000 for the building of the church of St. John the Baptist, Gannow.

In the bottom corner of the churchyard, shortly before reaching the lychgate, there are some eighteenth century graves. The burials commemorated here include the wife of Lawrence Simson (1746) and Jane (1749), the wife of John Chadwick, and their son Richard (1747).

Somewhere in the lower churchyard is the grave of Henry Wood, founder of the Wood Sermon. Dr. T.D. Whittaker's day book records that he was interred in the grounds of the chantry chapel on 1st November 1729. Anthony Weatherhead was also buried in this area of the churchyard.

Beside the lychgate, in an enclosure at the corner of the graveyard is the War Memorial, which was erected on the site of two old cottages. When the memorial was erected, the village stocks were placed at the back of the enclosure. Previously they stood next to the lychgate.

Resuming our walk towards Todmorden, we pass the only remaining traces of the chantry chapel and a horse trough. We soon come to a gateway on the lefthand side of the road. This is the first of two entrances to the grounds of The Holme.

The house stands on part of the land which was granted to Kirkstall Abbey. In 1302 the land passed into the possession of William de Midlemore whose wife Margaret was the daughter of Gilbert de la Legh of Hapton and Cliviger. A Richard Quitacre or Whitaker is known to have been in Cliviger about 1350 but there is no evidence to show where he lived. Dr. T.D. Whitaker suggests that he may have married a daughter of the Midlemores and later inherited the estate.

The Whitaker family's long association with the district can be traced from the first recorded member, Thomas Whitaker, in 1431. The date when the family home was first built is not known but the original building would be constructed of timber. From a date over a fireplace it appears that the rebuilding in stone of the central part and the east wing was completed in 1603. The west wing was rebuilt of stone in 1717. The original timber structure contained at least one priest hole. A recess has recently been discovered over a kitchen doorway in the central part of the building; it may also have served as a place of concealment. The Whitakers supported the Roman Catholic faith throughout many years of religious intolerance. In 1586 Lawrence Whitaker of Holme was constrained to conform to the Church of England.

"The Holme"

The Rev. A. Master-Whitaker caught in a light-hearted moment at The Holme.

An extension to the north side of the house was built in the 1850's. At the same time a porch was added to the main entrance. Magnificent stables, which also contained blacksmith's and joiner's workshops, were erected to the rear of the hall. These have now been converted into a bungalow. A feature of the main staircase is a beautiful stained glass window which overlooks the half-landing. Much of the glass was recovered from Whalley Abbey by Dr. T.D. Whitaker. The restored window includes a panel bearing the Whitaker family crest.

Like many old houses The Holme is reputed to be haunted. Mr. Eric Halstead, a resident for many years, believes that there are two friendly spirits within the house. One wears a monk's habit and is said to be Milo, one of two Whitakers who served at Whalley Abbey. He may have lived here in secrecy after the Dissolution. His body may have been walled up somewhere in the house, as on his death it would have been difficult to acknowledge his existence and bury him in the normal manner. The second ghost is that of a young girl with long fair hair. "The Lady in White' has recently been seen to walk across a room and pass through an enormous cupboard which blocks off a doorway leading to the main staircase!

The Whitaker family resided at The Holme for six centuries and each generation appears to have been highly respected. Three very distinguished members of the family were Dr. William Whitaker, Alexander Whitaker and Dr. Thomas Dunham Whitaker.

William was born at The Holme in 1548 and received his early education under the Master of Burnley Grammar School, William Hartgreave. After studying with his uncle, Alexander Nowell D.D. who was Dean of St. Paul's, London, he studied with great distinction at Cambridge Univerisity. At the age of 31 he was appointed Regius Professor of Divinity at Cambridge. Dr. Whitaker was a great champion of Protestantism. He died in 1595 and was buried in Trinity College, Cambridge. According to the records, Queen Elizabeth was said to be intent on buying his library in order to help his dependants but apparently never did so.

Whitakers were among the early settlers in North America. Alexander, the second son of Dr. William Whitaker was involved with the Virginia Company which settled at Jamestown. He became known as 'The Apostle of Virginia' and performed the baptism of the well known Red Indian princess, Pocahontas.

Dr. Thomas Dunham Whitaker was a great historian who was responsible for the building of St. John's Church. Born at Rainham, Norfolk in 1759, he was brought to live at The Holme the following year and eventually inherited the estate in 1782. Dr. Whitaker was a fine scholar who produced three important works, the histories of Whalley, Craven and Richmond. He was involved in the excavations of the ruins of Whalley Abbey and Ribchester.

Interior porch doors, The Holme.

The Holme contains some fine pieces of furnitu
Detail of the carving on a sideboard.

The Holme. Understood to have been made locally this bed was bought and taken to America when many of the contents of the house were put up for sale.

One of the most significant and unique items of the Roman period was found at Ribchester. This ceremonial helmet and mask is now in the possession of the British Museum. A replica of the helmet is displayed at the museum in Ribchester. It is understood that the helmet was discovered when being kicked around by a child and was then brought to the attention of Dr. Whitaker.

Between the years 1784 and 1799 Dr. Whitaker did much to enhance the beauty of the valley. The woodland areas which now clothe the formerly bare and rocky valley resulted from his efforts. Altogether he was responsible for the planting of 422,000 trees. The planting of 64,000 larch trees, carefully protected from cattle and sheep, lead to Dr. Whitaker being awarded a gold medal by The Society of Arts. Several pathways were laid down. These afforded the family many interesting views and later generations added to the paths, providing steps, embankments, bridges and handrails.

Within a few yards of the first entrance to The Holme a subway passes beneath the road to the fields across the way. This was one of the two tunnels built by Thomas Hordern Whitaker. It allowed the family access to Holme Station and Dodbottom Wood without leaving their estate. By using both tunnels it was possible to walk a circuit of several miles of woodland in complete privacy. A short distance further along the road, just before the entrance to Berrils Green Farm on the left, the second subway passes under the road. Through here the Whitakers were able to reach the woods surrounding their fish ponds higher up the Calder.

In the more tranquil days of the nineteenth century, the sylvan setting of Berrils Green inspired the following lines

"Who would not walk at early dawn,
By Birl's Green Farm, in spring alone,
When Phoebus rays are seen to spread,
'Mong budding trees with spouters red,
In winter too, when snow is seen,
To mix with every varied green –
And when the mountains silent stream,
Is hid for weeks, to stop and dream".

The large upstairs window of the farmhouse is a handloom weaver's window. It allowed extra light for weaving and this particular example is one of the finest of its type in East Lancashire.

Many former handloom weaver's cottages still stand, especially in outlying districts of Burnley such as Briercliffe and Worsthorne. A large number were built in The Weaver's Golden Age. In this twelve year period at the end of the eighteenth century the average wages of the weaver reached £1 a week. Usually weavers' cottages had one large room downstairs where two looms were normally to be found standing on the flagged floor. In addition there would be a small scullery. Stone steps led upstairs to another large chamber. This was also used for weaving, allowing barely enough room for the family to sleep between the looms.

After 1815 wages and piece rates were cut and weavers' families experienced great hardship. Mr. Fielden of the Todmorden textile family, collected information regarding handloom weavers in the period 1831-33. Cliviger families had an average weekly wage of 10s. 3½d or 3s. 3d per worker. This amount allowed 1s. 10d for each member of the family. Rent, fuel and candles accounted for 2d per person which left 1s. 8d for food and clothing. This was believed to be adequate for the requirements of a family. In nearby Burnley the Select Vestry would not allow relief for any family unless their average income fell below 1s. 6d per head.

It is only a short step further to Pot Oven Farm which lies on the opposite side of the road from Berrils Green Farm. Old Pot Ovens, as it was formerly known, was one of the centres of the Cliviger pottery industry. Rural potteries of this type thrived throughout the country, supplying the needs of each locality. The improving transport systems of the last century enabled better wares to be brought in from the large pottery towns and the increased competition gradually killed off the small manufacturers.

The products of the different rural potteries were very similar and the surviving examples of Cliviger pottery are typical of the wares of that period. The pots are in the form of red-ware with a deep yellow, lead glaze. They are often decorated with slip trailing and sgraffito (a technique of scraping to reveal the colour beneath). Cliviger earthenware can be seen at Towneley Hall. Domestic items, such as bread mugs, are displayed in the kitchen. More decorative pieces are exhibited in the nearby Craft Museum.

Numerous sherds have been turned up around Robin Cross Hill and Pot Oven Farm, testifying to considerable quantities of pottery being produced. Written information concerning the potteries is scarce, save for a few references to earthenware manufacturers in directories and census returns.

It is possible that someone who had learnt his trade at Robin Cross Hill began his own business at Pot Oven Farm in the latter half of the eighteenth century. The Baines Directory of 1824 lists James Walmesley as an earthenware manufacturer here. James was still living at the farm in 1841, and had at that time ten children, seven of whom were boys. By the time of the 1851 Census the business appears to have closed down as there is no reference to potters at Pot Oven.

The items made at Pot Oven appear to have been mainly domestic wares with a few decorative pieces. Jugs of various sizes, stewpots, baking mugs, bowls, flower pots and flower pot saucers were likely products. It is understood that a large jug, a cider *birling* (birl: to pour out), has been pieced together from sherds dug from a tip behind the farm.

After passing Pot Oven Farm the road remains straight for a little over a quarter of a mile. An area of woodland, which lay beyond the field on the right-hand side of the road, has recently been cut down. This was Fish Pond Plantation. The clearing of the woodland allows a glimpse of the Whitakers' two remaining fish ponds, once the haunt of the heron. Formerly there were three ponds along the course of the Calder but the uppermost was drained and filled in some years ago. A fourth pond lies behind The Holme in the woodland of Green's

Clough. The sluice has fallen into disrepair and the pond only contains water after periods of prolonged heavy rain.

At the head of the upper fish pond there is evidence of an old dam which, together with an area of marshy ground behind, indicates the former presence of another pond. This, according to the 6 inch map of 1848, was Furnace Dam. Water from there flowed along a goit, which could be traced through the wood.

A smelt mill with water-powered bellows was built by Richard Towneley to serve the nearby Thieveley lead mines. The mill was probably located upstream of Pot Oven Farm on the opposite side of the river.

Ore from the mines would be brought to the mill down Blackgate, a packhorse trail, which passed the workings on its descent from Deerplay Moor. The line of this former trade route can be followed from the Thieveley Farm track by tracing a sunken pathway which winds its way down the slope. The depth of routeways like this was increased during periods of bad weather when animals hoofs reduced the surface to a quagmire. Often it was necessary to dig out the mud which was then piled on either side of the track. Towards the bottom of the slope this problem was overcome by the provision of a stone lined ginnel which ensured a safe foothold for the horses. After fording the Calder the packhorses climbed towards Lightbirks on the opposite side of the valley. Another short section of sunken routeway can be seen above the old quarry, close to the farm road. Coal and timber from Lightbirks was supplied to the lead mines.

Experienced smelters travelled about the countryside to the various mines. Smelting at Cliviger would be carried out two or three times a year. It was customary to have four men carrying out the smelting process. Two skilled men worked at the furnace. A labourer stoked the fire and was responsible for loading ore into the furnace. The fourth man prepared the ore for smelting and poured the molten lead into moulds, later adding the mark of the smelt mill. A fother (19½ hundredweight) of lead would be produced in the course of a day's smelting. In 1630 the ten hour operation earned the smelter five shillings.

On the far side of the fields, to the left of the road, an old track leads from Berrils Green Farm to Copy Bottom. Beside the track are two old quarries which were sources of ashlar and rubble. The larger of the two, Steen Delph, was worked in the last century and operations ceased about 70 years ago. It is remembered to have been of considerable depth but was later filled in with waste material from Copy Pit.

24

At the end of the straight section the road bends to the left on the approach to the cottages at Copy Bottom. A few yards before we reach the cottages the track from Berrils Green and Steen Delph joins the main road. It seems likely that this track marks the line of the original turnpike road of 1759 which passed to the rear of Berrils Green Farm and then directly in front of The Holme. The route of the road which we have walked between Holme Chapel and Copy Bottom, was determined by diversions from the road of 1759.

In December 1782 a meeting of the Burnley and Halifax Trust granted Dr. T.D. Whitaker the sum of sixteen guineas. This was to help meet the cost of *diverting and turning the road at his own expense from a place called Birrits (Berrils) Green Gate to the middle of the lane near Holmes Chapel, both in Cliviger, and for making a new road and fence there to the satisfaction of the surveyor of the road.* Between 1813 and 1820 further diversions were undertaken to improve stretches of the road between Cross o' the Dean and Bullshead.

The diversion of the road in 1782 may help to explain the strange action of William, the father of Dr. T.D. Whitaker, eight years earlier. A toll house and bar, which was erected near Todmorden in 1774, was destroyed later in the year by the Rev. Whitaker. At a time when mob violence occured against newly erected turnpikes, this was the only incident of its kind to be mentioned in the records of the Burnley and Halifax Trust.

Perhaps a dispute arose out of Mr. Whitaker's desire to have the road moved away from the frontage of The Holme, for his behaviour is difficult to understand. As a cleric from a respected family and also a trustee of the company, he committed a crime which could have earned him a severe punishment. In 1728 Parliament had introduced public whipping and three months in the common gaol for this crime. This act proved ineffective and later the death penalty was introduced for acts against the turnpikes.

Reports in journals of the period describe *The Black Acts* in Hertfordshire in 1735, the following year in Middlesex and in Somerset during 1749. Mobs with blackened faces, and disguised in women's clothing, gathered at night to destroy the toll bars.

Mr. Whitaker appears to have been rather fortunate, for at a meeting of the Trustees at Halifax in February 1775 the clerk was instructed to *aquaint him of his trespassing by Destroying a Barr erected at or near Todmorden, and to settle the Matter without any further Trouble.*

We walk 50 or 60 yards back along the track from the junction with the road. Here there is a rectangular enclosure of trees on the right-hand side. The 1848 six inch map shows a "Pottery Factory" of considerable size on the site. No mention of this particular pottery is made in directories or census returns of the period and it is possible that the workers were largely farmers' wives and children employed on a seasonal basis.

The Burnley Gazette of 20th June 1885 has an interesting account of a ramble through Cliviger. According to the writer, pot making was carried out on a large scale at the factory about 1840. He mentions black glossy pots being manufactured which were *in common use in every household in this and other localities.* There is no evidence of any black pottery from the Cliviger area and earthenware sherds found in this vicinity are of the traditional red-ware.

The writer of the article recounts a fascinating story in connection with the pottery.

I have been told that this was the place to which a man came from Bacup for pots, with cart and horse. He had with him a boy with a new suit of clothes on, the trousers were kept up by being fastened to some bell buttons on the jacket. 'Tis said an old woman who was thought to be a witch took a glance at the lad, when all the buttons fell off, causing his breeches to slip down to his feet. This put the lad in great trouble, causing tears to flow freely, when another look from the woman caused the buttons to be bound up, and fix anew to the place from which they had fallen. Now this was a most wonderful feat, such as we have not the pleasure of seeing in our day. Shortly the lad wiped the lingering tears from off his cheek, seeing that all was right again. No doubt he would say "Aw'll tell me mother when aw get whome".

The approach to Copy Bottom.

The row at Copy Bottom consists of former miners' cottages. The buildings, like those of Croft Houses at Holme Chapel, have shot-stone walling which indicates that they were erected at the turn of the eighteenth century. Three larger houses once stood at the far end of the row. These were demolished in the late 1960s.

A short distance further along the road, on the same side as the cottages, is the entrance to the former Copy Pit. Several old pits existed in this area of the valley. 'Bee hive' or 'bell' pits, higher up the valley side at Cartridge Pasture, may have been worked from the late seventeenth century. The 'bee hive' pit had a narrow shaft which was sunk about 30 feet down to find the coal, which was cut away around the bottom of the shaft thus creating a roughly circular chamber. When the pit had been excavated to a diameter of about 30 feet it was abandoned as there was a danger of the unsupported roof collapsing.

Copy Pit opened in 1852, although there had been earlier attempts to work the coal at this site. When worked by the Cliviger Coal and Coke Co., the mine possessed a unique 'back to back' winding system with two lift cages operating side by side in a single shaft. At Copy the cages occupied shafts situated at opposite ends of the winding house, thus resulting in the headgear standing back to back.

In the latter half of last century, there was much discontent among miners concerning the method of payment by measure. The miners were paid for the number of tubs they filled with coal. As early as 1860 there had been attempts to bring in payment by weight, but local colliery owners and miners had agreed not to adopt the new scheme. In 1876 a strike occured at Copy Pit when the owners introduced new tubs. The replacement tubs were considered to be larger than those previously used. As the miners were to be paid at the old rate they calculated that they would be losing 9½d on every six tubs. In 1901 payment by weight was finally agreed upon and checkweighmen were appointed to ensure that miners were correctly paid.

In later years Copy Pit was worked as a 'drift' and was entered by a tunnel driven horizontally into the hillside. The miners were presented with problems due to intensive faulting of the rock strata. Often, when a fault was encountered, the coal seam was as much as 40 feet higher or lower on the far side of the fracture. The colliery closed in March, 1965. The site has recently been landscaped and young pine, spruce and ash have been planted.

A bee-hive or bell pit.

Cliviger pottery.

The original school building and the old churchyard gate.

The octagonal cupola.

The grave of William Smith, a Cliviger potter.

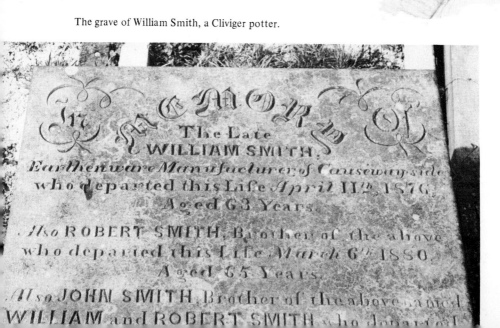

In **Memory** of
The Late
WILLIAM SMITH,
Earthenware Manufacturer of Causewayside
who departed this Life April 11th 1876,
Aged 63 Years.

Also ROBERT SMITH, Brother of the above
who departed this Life March 6th 1850,
Aged 65 Years.

Also JOHN SMITH, Brother of the above named
WILLIAM and ROBERT SMITH

Holme Chapel.

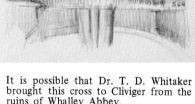

The Chantry Chapel.

It is possible that Dr. T. D. Whitaker brought this cross to Cliviger from the ruins of Whalley Abbey.

The lychgate, St. John's Church.

The former railway siding and loading bay at Copy Pit. In the centre is the Whitaker's upper fish pond.

Alongside the footpath, by the former mine entrance, is a stone retaining wall. At this point there was a familiar landmark for motorists going through the valley. A loading gantry passed above the road to the colliery's railway siding on the opposite side. In the last century a row of coke ovens was situated close to here on the left hand side of the road. The *'Burnley Gazette'* article of 1885 describes the ovens as *"not being used for many years and now lying in ruins"*.

Leaving the site of the colliery, we pass Cross o' th' Dean Farm. On old maps the name is given as *Crossing of Dean* (Valley) which gives a clue to the probable derivation of the name. A pack horse route can be clearly traced through the old lime workings of the Shedden Valley. From the Long Causeway it probably descended into the Cliviger Valley and "crossed the dean", before climbing back to the moorland heights at Green's Clough, Portsmouth, from where it led to Rochdale. This route would avoid the need to ford water-courses when they were in full spate.

We proceed along a 350 yard straight section of the road. Parallel on the right is the railway line which is descending from its 749 foot summit at Copy. At the beginning of the straight section, stone abutments and a girder carry a pipe across the railway. The pipe was installed to provide water for the boilers and the bath house at Copy Pit. Additionally, the water, which was obtained from a spring rising high on the hillside, was supplied to Cross o' th' Dean Farm and the cottages at Copy Bottom.

This part of the valley, on the approach to Windy Bridge (locally 'Brig'), is called Calderhead. As we walk towards the bridge, which carries the road across the railway cutting, we cross a major Pennine watershed. A watershed is an imaginery boundary line separating the headwaters of different river systems. Within a short distance of Calderhead are the sources of the two Calders. The Lancashire Calder rises below the rocks of Thieveley Scout. It eventually flows into the Ribble beyond Whalley and then drains into the Irish Sea. The Yorkshire Calder flows into the Aire and by way of the Humber Estuary into the North Sea. The name Calder occurs frequently in this country. It is proabably Celtic in origin, derived from the roots 'cul' or 'col' (narrow or cold) and 'dwr' (water).

At 'Windy Brig' there is a good view south-eastwards down the valley. From here we can see the contrast in the landscape caused by the Cliviger Valley Fault. To the southwest is the escarpment of Millstone Grit rocks, formed from strata which dip gently from the horizontal. To the northeast are the Coal Measures of the downthrown side of the fault. These rocks dip more steeply towards the bottom of the valley, thus encouraging movement of the beds. To the left of the railway can be seen the typical hummocky ground which results from landslipping of this nature.

To the right of the railway is Ratten Clough Farm which takes its name from an impressive cleft in the precipitous valley side. At this point the infant Yorkshire Calder falls sharply from its moorland source due to over-deepening of the Cliviger Valley by glacial melt-water. As it tumbles to the main valley floor, the stream forms two sizeable waterfalls, the lower one being 90 feet high.

1967. Heavy freight locomotive number 48218 passes beneath the pipe which supplied water to Copy Pit.

The lower waterfall, Ratten Clough.

In 1947, persistent heavy rain lubricated opencast mining debris on Heald Moor, above the clough. On 18th October thousands of tons of mud cascaded down the clough. The mud flow spread across a considerable stretch of road, blocking it to a depth of six feet, and finally came to rest just before the railway line.

The valley side beyond Ratten Clough was a source of fireclay for the Towneley Coal and Fireclay Co. A series of wooden shutes were erected down the face of the scarp to facilitate the loading of wagons at road level. During the last war the workings were utilised for the storing of high explosives. Heavy steel doors protected the entrance to the store.

From our viewpoint at 'Windy Brig', it is just possible to make out the gable end of New Hey, a farmhouse to the left of the railway track. Hidden from view above the farm, are outcrops of the Middle Coal Measures. The escarpments, which are formed by Coal Measure Sandstones, can be seen from the lay-by near the foot of Ratten Clough.

The first escarpment above the farm is Riddle Scout, an outcrop of the famous Arley Coal Seam. The shales above the coal seam were the source of a medieval ironstone industry. It is likely that the occurence of red iron deposits in the locality gave rise to the early name 'Ruddle Scout' from the Anglo-Saxon word 'rud' (red).

The iron mine was explored by Captain Aitken during the last century. His findings were recorded in a Manchester Geological Society Paper – *"On the Discovery of an Ancient Iron Mine in Cliviger"*. According to his description the mine consisted of a series of drifts driven into the hillside. As the tunnels had been skilfully cut and the roof was sound, the Captain was able to progress about 300 feet into the mine. The four foot square roads had enabled the miners to extract valuable ironstone from four bands which varied in thickness from half an inch to 5 or 6 inches. The drifts have long since been blocked off.

It appeared from his account that the ore was not smelted locally, as no 'bloomeries' had been found in Cliviger. (A bloomery is a furnace for making iron ore into blooms – masses of iron in an intermediate stage of manufacture). The nearest furnaces of this type were at Brunshaw, Dulesgate (Walsden), Hebden Bridge and in the Rossendale Valley. Captain Aitken reported large spoil heaps at the entrance to the mine. As large accumulations of calcined brick-red shale were to be seen there, it seems likely that a small bloomery did exist on the site.

The mine was worked in early times before the disappearance of much of the local woodland, which was sadly depleted by the beginning of the sixteenth century. Mention is made of an important discovery of ironstone at Cliviger in 1305. Several years later the records of the Lancashire and Cheshire Honors of Henry de Lacy show *"Clivachure iron sold for ten weeks – 6s. 6d"*.

At the same period coal was extracted from the adjacent Arley seam, one of the earliest known instances of coal mining in Lancashire.

We leave 'Windy Brig' and walk back along the road which bends to the left after passing Copy Bottom. At the point where it begins to curve in the opposite direction, a gate on the left-hand side of the road allows access to a track. We follow the track as it wends its way towards the railway, noticing to our left the levelled area which marks the site of the upper fish pond. After passing under the railway, the track skirts a small wood. As we walk towards Thieveley Scout the area of crags and wooded slopes immediately confronting us is Earl's Bower. We continue to ascend the track which now bends back on itself to run parallel with the crags.

The escarpment of Thievely is very impressive and was caused by the displacement of the rock strata along the Cliviger Valley Fault. In contrast to the relatively soft Middle Coal Measures on the north-east side of the valley, Thievely is composed of craggy rocks belonging to the upper section of the Millstone Grits. Three distinctive bands of sandstone can be seen in the face of the scarp. For a short distance along the base, Haslingden Flagstones outcrop. The Woodhead Hill Rock forms the crest of the scarp and just below is the outcrop of the Rough Rock. These upper bands, eroded by seasonal streams flowing down the rock face, have a buttressed appearance.

As the track continues to climb, the wall on the left ends and another starts on the right. In the valley between the track and Thieveley Scout, there is a 250 yard long shelf of land. The slope on the edge of the shelf is convex and indicates a piling up of landslipped material. An ancient bog-burst, similar to the postwar one at Ratten Clough, probably resulted in mud and earth from Thieveley Pike flowing down the valley behind the shelf. On encountering the more gentle slope at the foot of the valley, the mud settled, allowing consolidation to take place as the liquid content seeped away.

On the right of the track, just before the gate at the top, stood Thieveley Farm, once a popular picnic spot for visitors to the district. The farm stood empty for many years after the last war and it eventually fell into a dangerous state of repair and had to be pulled down.

Mr. and Mrs. Little with daughter Edna, on horseback, at Thievely Farm.

Until the 1930's, family groups, Sunday school and works' parties walked from Burnley and 'o'er t' tops' from Bacup and Weir for a day's outing. Others arrived by train and alighted at Holme Station.

Mr. W. Nuttall, who left the farm in 1924 to run the Deerplay Inn, and his successors the Little family, provided facilities for the visitors. Minerals and sweets were on sale in a small shop at the farm. There was a dining room and jugs of tea were available for picknickers. To the rear of the farm, on the flat surface of the ancient mud flow, were the children's amusements. Swings and roundabouts were erected there and in addition the youngsters could enjoy a ride on one of the two donkeys.

Basically worked as a hill sheep farm, Thieveley also had a herd of 20 cattle. Pigs were also kept and each year two pigs were slaughtered to provide home cured bacon. Together with butter, cheese and eggs, this ensured that the farm was largely self sufficient. During World War I the surplus cheese sold particularly well and there was a waiting list of hopeful buyers.

Improving road transport and easy access to the west coast resorts led to a decline in the local 'outing'. After the Little family left Thieveley in 1932 the new owner confined his interest to farming.

A short, steep climb beside the wall, to the left of the gate, takes us up Dean Scout. On the side of the ridge, which faces Thieveley Scout, is Beacon Rock. Like Pendle Hill and Blacko, this was one of the local sites, part of a country-wide chain, where a beacon fire would be lit in times of national peril or celebration. Events such as the sighting of the Spanish Armada caused the kindling of the fires. In 1977 the site was once more put to its traditional use to celebrate the Queen's Jubilee Year.

Beacon Rock exhibits a feature called false bedding which presents the geologist with evidence of the prevailing conditions at the time when the rock was deposited. The layers or beds in which sedimentary rocks were laid down are often apparent in an outcrop. False (or current) bedding is set at an angle to the true beds. It is caused by the sediments coming to rest on an underwater slope, such as the edge of a sand bar, and is typical of deposition in an estuary.

On crossing the ridge and looking down the opposite side, we can see an area of hummocky ground. Two separate attempts to mine lead on a small scale took place hereabouts, but each failed within a few years.

The important lead mining areas of England were in The Mendips, Derbyshire and the northern Pennines. In these regions the rock structures produced favourable conditions for the existence of galena (lead ore). The rock structure in Cliviger was of a different nature and was unsuitable for large, workable deposits of ore. This fact was noted in a letter written to John Slaney in April 1631 by Thomas Braye, who wrote-

'This mine att Clevager is contrarie to our mines in our country, for itt lies in the greetstone, and our mines are all in the limestone, and mingled with cauke and keavell as we call itt which makes our oare work better than this will do of itt selfe, for this lieth in a black shale and is very pure'.

The deposits of lead occured along the Thieveley Lead Mine Fault, a fracture in the rock structure, which runs from east to west across the slopes of Deerplay Moor. It is possible that the galena was first found in the Bronze Age, as fragments were discovered in a burial urn of that period, found two miles to the north of Thieveley, at Moseley Height.

Godfrey Mercer of Rochdale discovered the ore about the year 1626. He and several others worked the lead vein until the intervention of the Duchy of Lancaster. As owner of the land it appointed several people, including Ralph Highley and William Butler, to work the mines for the Crown.

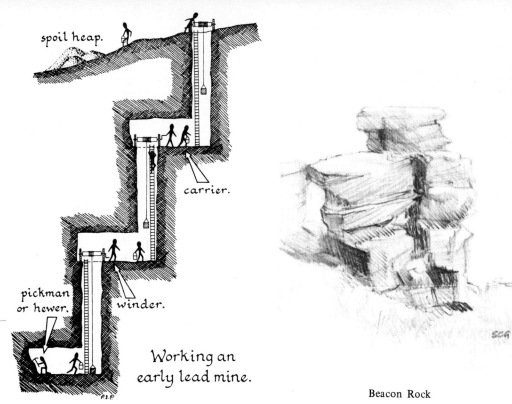

spoil heap.

carrier.

pickman or hewer.

winder.

Working an early lead mine.

Beacon Rock

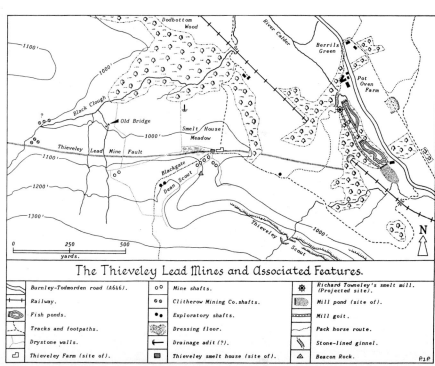

The Thieveley Lead Mines and Associated Features.

	Burnley-Todmorden road (A646).	○○ Mine shafts.		Richard Towneley's smelt mill. (Projected site).
	Railway.	◑○ Clitherow Mining Co. shafts.		Mill pond (site of).
	Fish ponds.	●● Exploratory shafts.		Mill goit.
	Tracks and footpaths.	Dressing floor.		Pack horse route.
	Drystone walls.	← Drainage adit (?).		Stone-lined ginnel.
	Thieveley Farm (site of).	▨ Thieveley smelt house (site of).	△	Beacon Rock.

In 1629 members of the local gentry were commissioned to inquire into the workings of the mine, to determine whether the profits could be expected to make a useful contribution to the finances of Charles I, which were embarrassingly low. Following the questioning of many witnesses, it appeared that the mines were far from efficient. Apart from the employees of Highley and Butler, most of the witnesses spoke optimistically about the richness of the lead vein. It would appear that there was an attempt to discredit Highley and Butler, but as the mines later proved to be unsuccessful, it is reasonable to assume that they had assessed the situation correctly. Ultimately the Chancellor of the Duchy of Lancaster appointed members of the local gentry to work the mines, under the direction of Roger Kenyon.

In August 1630 Kenyon visited Derbyshire in order to study the mining methods employed there. His report gave an excellent account of the early methods of mining lead ore.

A shaft was never sunk continuously downwards but descended by a series of steps. After reaching a depth of approximately 50 feet, a tunnel was excavated horizontally for roughly 20 feet and then the shaft continued downwards. By a succession of such steps the maximum depth of the mine was attained. The Derbyshire mines varied in depth from 120 feet to 240 feet, exceptional ones being sunk to a depth of 300 feet. By comparison the deepest of the Cliviger mines was about 200 feet. Some of the smaller Cliviger diggings were simple bell pits.

A 'pickman' or 'hewer' worked in the deepest part of the mine and was assisted by a 'carrier', who transported the ore to a basket. A 'winder' raised the basket of ore to the level above. A second carrier moved the ore to the base of the next shaft and the process was repeated until the load reached the surface where it was deposited.

Ore was not weighed but was measured by the 'dish'. This consisted of a wooden dish measuring 28 inches by 6 inches by 4 inches. (Fifty dishes were equivalent to a ton). In the period 16th January 1630 to 24th November 1632 the total ore extracted amounted to 81 tons and 34 dishes.

The smelting process was difficult; despite new hand-bellows which were bought specially from *'One Carre, a man famous for that trade'*. As this equipment did not solve the problem it was decided to build a smelting mill by the River Calder. The new mill was financed by Richard Towneley but could hardly have repaid him. By 1634 the Commissioners had become discouraged by the continual losses, so the mines were abandoned.

Robert Hartley, tenant of Thieveley Farm complained to the Duchy of Lancaster about the smoke from the smelting process which *". . . destroy the growth of all herbes and seedes sown in a garden neare adioninge to the same house, and also destroyeth and taketh awaie the colour and vertue both of grasse and corne".* This was one of seven points which Hartley raised in his petition. His complaint was noted in the Resolutions of the Council (3rd December 1629) when it was decided that if Hartley or any other person had just cause the Commissioners would recompense them.

In 1628 Thieveley lead was supplied to the Towneley estate. Four and a half tons were provided for roofing.

A second attempt to work the mines began in 1755. *The Clitherow Mining Co.,* or *The Clitherow Co. of Miners* as it was also known, was set up with the aim of developing mines in the Honor of Clitheroe. The Company, which was later known as *The Mine Adventurers' Co.,* had an office at Dunnockshaw. Exploratory digging and mining was carried out at a dozen or so sites in East Lancashire. In addition to Cliviger operations were undertaken at Gambleside, Whin Hill Clough, Dunnockshaw, Thornybank Clough, Goodshaw Hill, Cribden, Rising Bridge, Baxenden, Pendle Rise and Worston.

In Cliviger the Thieveley site appears to have been extended by mines opened in Black Clough. According to an account in the *Transactions of the Manchester Geological Society* (Vol. XIII, 1876) ten unfilled shafts could be traced there. Six workings, together with a dressing floor, were to be found on the right bank of the stream. A second dressing floor and the remaining shafts were located further up the valley on the opposite side of the stream.

Once again the venture failed, and the workings in Cliviger were abandoned in 1766. Although the mines have long since been filled in, a little careful exploration of the immediate vicinity will reveal traces of the industry.

Alongside the former pack horse route, Blackgate, which gradually ascends the side of Dean Scout, a number of hollows show the positions of the old shafts. Below the track, beside the fence, patches of bare earth mark the former dressing floor where spoil from the mines was dumped. Small fragments of galena can be found here. Barytes, a heavy, pinkish mineral, which is often associated with lead ore deposits, can also be found. Unfortunately, following visits by parties of students, the mineral specimens have become rather sparse.

An adit, which served to drain the mines, was located nearby. According to the mining company's records it was driven into the hillside about 180 feet below the entrance to the workings. An open ditch running down Smelt House Meadow into Black Clough is the likely course of the adit.

In the first tributary clough, above the top of Dodbottom Wood, are the remains of a small bridge. Stone abutments, originally supporting a timber platform, were almost certainly built to carry a cart track leading to the Clitherow Mining Company's shafts, higher up Black Clough.

Towards the head of Black Clough there is a small colliery waste heap, the only remaining trace of mining operations which took place there immediately before World War II. Coal was extracted from Black Clough drift mine for about fifteen years. A ginny track carried the coal across the moorland to Deerplay Colliery.

From the Thieveley Farm site we can enjoy a fine view south-eastwards along the valley; the gorge-like nature of the valley contrasts sharply with the comparatively flat moorland through which it was carved by the immense volume of glacial meltwater.

In the opposite direction lie the Burnley basin and Pendle Hill. To the north, in the valley below, is Holme Chapel and it is in this direction that we now make our way. A vaguely defined field path leads down to a stile on the edge of Dodbottom Wood. Entering the wood we walk alongside a fence for a short distance and leave the shelter of the trees by a small gate. A steep, stepped path descends to the road below. We follow the road down to the railway where it passes under two bridges.

The first of these was constructed as part of the Whitakers' system of walks. The route from The Holme emerged from a subway through the railway embankment and was then carried above the public road by the attractive stone footbridge. At this point the family would either enter Holme Station by a private entrance or continue into Dodbottom Wood. A feature of the woodland walk was a 50 yard long 'tunnel' which had been cut through the dense rhododendron bushes. A footbridge carried the path below the waterfall at the head of the wood, and from there it returned to the bottom of the clough, down the opposite bank of the stream.

Private subway beneath the railway line, close to the site of Holme Station.

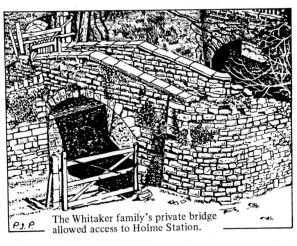

The Whitaker family's private bridge allowed access to Holme Station.

Holme Station. Workmen clearing wreckage after the accident of 1907.

Holme Station at the turn of the century.

Holme Station following the accident of 1907.

A short distance beyond the railway underpass there is a small gate in the wall on the left. This was the public entrance to Holme Station, which was a well known stopping point for visitors to the village and the surrounding beauty spots. The development of regular 'bus services through the valley' caused a decline in the number of passengers, and the station was closed in 1930.

In September 1907 a spectacular accident occurred at the station. A heavy goods train, en route from Normanton to Liverpool, stopped at the Todmorden end of Holme Tunnel. On restarting, it appears that a coupling snapped and 27 wagons became separated. The wagons gradually picked up speed on the gradient and began to career down the track, rapidly overtaking the engine and the remaining wagons. Although the driver spotted the danger and tried to increase speed, a crash took place just as Holme Station was reached. Several wagons jumped the rails and three or four swept along the down platform, reducing the station building to matchwood. William Pim, the temporary station-master, was sitting in his office and received fatal injuries. Fortunately, apart from Mr. Pim, the station was deserted at the time of the accident.

Our way now turns to the right away from the railway. At the bend a farm gate allows access to a track, running parallel to the railway, leading to the curiously named Jumb Hole Farm. The name suggests a connection with water, perhaps referring to a well close by. Another possibility is that the name is derived from a deep pool on the nearby Calder. Two examples of the name existed on the Brun. One was a favourite haunt of fishermen, near the college buildings on Ormerod Road. P.G. Hammerton, the critic and engraver, mentions a Jumb Hole located close to his home at The Hollins.

Beside the farm the footpath crosses the railway. At this point stood a fine example of a Lancashire and Yorkshire Railway warning notice. Regrettably this has recently been removed.

We walk along Station Road back to Holme Chapel. The stream from Black Clough flows alongside as it makes its way to join the Calder. Drainage water from Deerplay Colliery is channelled into the head of the clough and for many years the discoloured water has left an orange coating on all that it touched. As we pass the confluence of the two streams, we can see the effect of the pollution on the previously clear waters of the Calder, an effect that was formerly apparent downstream as the river flowed through Towneley Holmes. Recently, conditions have improved and hopefully, in the near future, the Calder will revert to its natural state.

At the end of the lane we return to the Burnley-Todmorden road and turn to the right. Situated at the corner there is a small garden and a shelter. On this site stood a blacksmith's workshop. The 200 year old smithy had often been the meeting place for the locals to enjoy a casual conversation. It was falling into ruin, so in 1949 it was demolished and the stones were used by voluntary labour to create an open air "forum". The garden was officially opened the following year.

The back wall of the shelter bears a plaque with this inscription.

THIS BUILDING WAS ERECTED
VOLUNTARILY DURING 1949
FOR THE BENEFIT AND
COMFORT OF THE AGED.
A SHELTER FROM THE
STORM AND SUN.
A RESTING PLACE WHEN
WORK IS DONE.

A stone plinth stands in the centre of the lawn. A sundial, which was later smashed by vandals, was erected on the spot formerly occupied by the blacksmith's anvil.

Next to the garden are two houses, the further of the two being referred to locally as 'the schoolmaster's house'. The present building replaced two old cottages in 1890. The datestone was removed from the cottages and incorporated in the fabric of the new building. It bears the initials of T.A. Whitaker, together with the date 1707.

We now come to the Ram Inn with its interesting sign. It is possible that the painting represents a prize winning "tup" (ram) from one of the Lonk Sheepbreeders' first shows. A very old breed, the Lonk is the largest of the black-faced mountain sheep and is extremely hardy. It is the native sheep of the local area and, with the exception of a handful which are taken for cross-breeding elsewhere, is largely confined to East Lancashire. It may even owe its name to a corruption of "Lanky" sheep.

At the head of the board are symbols depicting different ranks of the Freemasons and these may indicate that a travelling lodge met here in earlier days. Formerly the nearest permanent lodges were situated at Accrington and Colne. The present sign carries the signature of Alf. Smith and is dated June 1958.

Like many of the old country inns The Ram would have come into existence as a room at a farm where the farmer or his wife sold home brewed ale as a sideline. An entry in the 1851 Census suggests that the inn was part of Plum Tree Farm, James Lancaster being listed as an inkeeper and farmer of 47 acres there. The Lancaster family were associated with The Ram for many years. The newspaper account of the accident at Holme Station in 1907 states that one of the first people to arrive at the scene was the landlord of the inn, Valentine Lancaster.

Plum Tree Farm belonged to the Whitaker estate. An old account book at The Holme records one year's rent for the Holme Chapel Inn for 1822. William Whitaker was a farmer of 22 acres and innkeeper. In the wall of the extension, alongside the rear entrance to the building, is a worn datestone on which can be made out T.A. Whitaker's initials and the date 1691. Presumably it was preserved when earlier buildings were demolished. The remaining farm buildings were pulled down to allow the car park to be extended in the mid 1950s.

It seems likely that the nearby smithy formerly belonged to the Whitaker estate. Baines' Directory of Lancashire, 1824 records Robert Whitaker as victualler and blacksmith at The Ram.

Holme Sheep Fair, the expert's opinion.

Holme Sheep Fair, a successful conclusion for an entrant in the sheepdog trials.

The fields close to The Ram are the venue of the Holme Sheep Fair which takes place annually in late September. It is one of the few survivors of the village fairs which were common in days gone by, and according to local tradition, the Holme Fair dates back to Elizabethan times.

The fairs were an important event in comparatively isolated rural communities. Held in the autumn, at the end of the farming year, they allowed the farmers to dispose of surplus livestock and crops, thus enabling them to buy seed and supplies for the following year. Town traders were able to bring their wares to a central point where people from the surrounding district had gathered. It was also customary at the fair to hire farm and domestic servants, often on a one year contract.

CLIVIGER SHOW AUG 7\09

Holme Sheep Fair, 1909.

The fair at Holme was primarily concerned with the buying and selling of sheep and also allowed the farmers to sort out stray animals. The sale of local sheep is now conducted at the modern Clitheroe auction mart, so the days when sheep pens lined the roadside for hundreds of yards are gone. However, the fair has become the annual show of the Lonk Sheepbreeders' Association and is well worth a visit. In addition to the judging of one of the country's oldest breeds of hill sheep there is the fascination of the sheep dog trials. Some of the finest dogs in Britain are put through their paces in the Holme competition. A further attraction is the gruelling fell race to the summit of Thieveley Pike and back.

The Sheep Fair of 1741 was the scene of a tragic incident. Lawrence Briercliffe, who farmed locally, took to drinking as a result of his marital problems and became a quarrelsome drunkard of the worst kind. His wife was brought up in a strict Church of England home and apparently a major factor in their constant arguments was her objection to Lawrence, a staunch Baptist, regularly travelling to Bacup where he attended the services of a *most popular preacher*, David Crossley.

On the occasion of the Sheep Fair, Lawrence and a friend were much the worse for drink and fell into heated argument. In a drunken rage Lawrence took hold of a curdle or churn staff and, to the horror of the bystanders, killed his unfortunate friend. Although instantly over-powered, he managed to break free and make good his escape.

Lawrence fled the district and is understood to have found his way to the naval yard of Portsmouth, where he enlisted as a sailor. Two attempts to put to sea resulted in the fleet returning to harbour through adverse weather conditions and Lawrence, with the blood of his friend on his conscience, became convinced that he was a "Jonah".

He jumped ship and quietly made his way back to his home at Portsmouth in Cliviger. There he made himself known to one of his farm hands, before going to live for a time in a cave at Dodbottom Wood. At length, believing that he had a chance of acquittal, he surrendered to the constable.

At the Lancaster Assizes of 1742 he was found guilty of the murder and was sentenced to death. Whilst awaiting execution the repentant Lawrence sent for Mr. Crossley. The Baptist preacher must have been a man of considerable stamina for he made the long journey to and from Lancaster on foot.

On 23rd May, 1742, following Lawrence's request, Mr. Crossley preached an open air funeral sermon on the site of Bacup Mechanic's Institute. At least 4,000 people attended. The sermon, when published, ran to 127 pages!

Here, within a short distance of the church, the Holme and the inn, each with its own fascinating link with the past, we conclude our second walk "All o'er t' Parish".

The Ram Inn in the early 1900's.

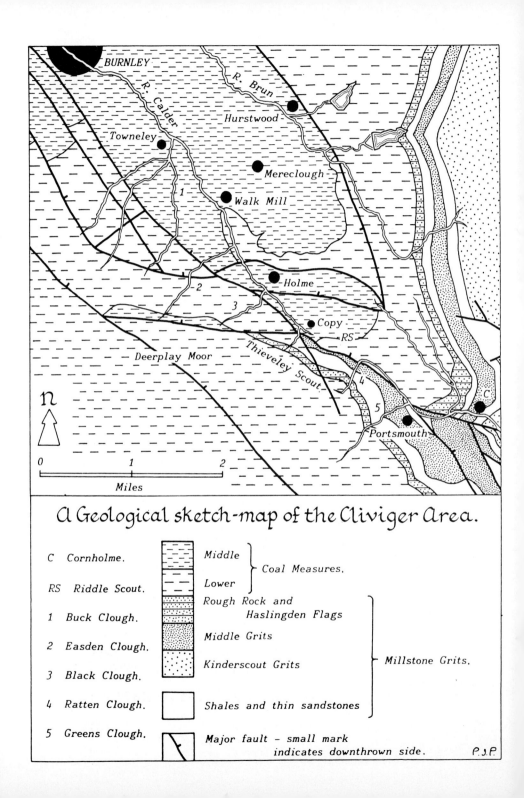

A Geological sketch-map of the Cliviger Area.

C   Cornholme.

RS   Riddle Scout.

1   Buck Clough.

2   Easden Clough.

3   Black Clough.

4   Ratten Clough.

5   Greens Clough.

Middle ⎫
Lower ⎬ Coal Measures.

Rough Rock and
       Haslingden Flags ⎫
Middle Grits ⎬ Millstone Grits.
Kinderscout Grits ⎭

Shales and thin sandstones

Major fault – small mark
     indicates downthrown side.

P.J.P.

GEOLOGY

Early historians suggested that the name Cliviger originated from a Saxon word "Clivvig" and referred to a rocky district. Whatever your vantage point in the Valley, you cannot fail to be aware of the impressive and imposing rock structures which prompted this theory. Not only do the rocks provide us with striking scenery, but they have also made an enormous contribution to the economic and social development of the Valley.

The rocks which make up the earth's crust have been formed over a period of some 4,600 million years. Throughout the earth's existence there has been a continual process of rock formation under various conditions.

Rocks can be separated into three groups according to their mode of origin.

Igneous rocks are formed from molten mixtures of material called magma, which is created in the intense heat of the mantle, deep below the surface of the earth. The composition of the magma, and the conditions under which it cools, largely determines the characteristics of the resulting rock. Magma, which forces its way to the earth's surface and erupts as lava, cools quickly and produces fine grained rocks such as basalt. Magma, which cools slowly beneath the ground, produces rocks of a coarser grain, probably the best known of this type being granite.

The physical appearance of the landscape around us is in a constant state of change. Generally these changes go unnoticed, taking place over extremely long periods of time. Weathering, the action of ice, snow, wind and rain, continually attacks and erodes existing rocks into small fragments. Many of the fragments are transported by glaciers, rivers and streams until they are eventually laid down as sediments on the ocean floors. The particles become compressed under successive deposits and harden into sedimentary rocks such as shale (or mudstone), sandstone, gritstone and limestone. Rocks of this type usually exhibit the well marked layers of deposition, which are referred to as bedding.

Metamorphic rocks make up the third group. These are rocks which were formed as igneous or sedimentary rocks. However at some stage since their formation, they have been altered in character by extremes of heat and/or pressure. Marble is the product of limestone which has been altered in this manner. The slate, which is to be seen on many local houses, was transformed from a soft shale by the effects of metamorphism.

The many different rocks, which occur in the crust, are placed on a geological time scale according to the order in which they were formed. Geological time is divided into twelve major periods, which have a well established order, although the actual dates of the periods cannot be defined exactly.

The rocks of the Cliviger Valley are sedimentary in origin and the particular phase of geological time in which they were laid down is known as the Carboniferous (coal forming) Age. The period began approximately 350 million years ago and lasted about 80 million years.

During the first half of the Carboniferous Age an invasion of the sea submerged all but a few parts of what is now the British Isles. It was a period of warm, clear-water seas in which many creatures flourished. The ooze, which accumulated on the sea bed, together with the remains of the sea creatures, formed the Carboniferous Limestone areas which are to be seen to the north and west of Pendle Hill.

In the latter half of the Carboniferous period there was a dramatic change in conditions which led to the formation of the rocks encountered in Cliviger. A vast continent then stretched northwards from Britain, and rivers flowing into this area from far to the north brought deposits which gradually filled in the open seas where the limestone oozes had accumulated. In a series of river deltas deposits of coarse grained sands and silts resulted in the formation of the Millstone Grit Series. Occasional invasions of the sea introduced layers of mud which hardened into bands of shale containing fossils of sea creatures (marine bands).

In the later stages of the Carboniferous Age a sedimentary basin had developed over much of Northern England and the Midlands. Shallow lagoons and marshes with predominantly brackish water resulted in the deposition of the Coal Measures. Varying conditions, repeated at intervals, produced a recurring sequence which is characteristic of the Coal Measure strata.

The sequence began with the deposits of sandstones, flagstones, siltstones and shales in open water areas. As the deposits built up above sea level, land plants gained a foothold and swampy forests grew up. The layers of peat, which were created by the decaying vegetation, ultimately changed to coal when later subjected to pressure deep below the surface of the earth.

Subsidence or renewed flooding of the area caused a new sequence of shale, siltstone, sandstone, seat-earth (in which the vegetation grew) and coal, which was repeated time and again, resulting in the formation of many coal seams of varying thicknesses.

Due to their sedimentary origin, the rocks of the Cliviger Valley would be laid down more or less horizontally, much like layers in a pile

A coal-forming swamp of the Carboniferous Period.

Fossil plants from a bore hole near Worsthorne. A fern leaf (left) and stems of Calamites (right).

Marine fossils. Dunbarella, a lamellibranch (above). The cephalopod, Gastrioceras (below).

A coal seam with band of fireclay beneath, Fish Pond Clough, Thieveley Scout.

of sandwiches. If they had remained in this state, it would have made life much simpler for the geologist and the miner. However, pressures and tensions within the earth's crust cause folding and faulting (cracking and dislocation) of the rocks, which makes the geological picture far more complicated.

The Cliviger Valley cuts across a major upfold, the Pennine Anticline, which, in the immediate area, runs in a north-easterly direction. The anticline is asymmetrical, the dip of the rock strata on the Lancashire side being steeper than the dip to the east.

The rock layers in the Cliviger Valley exhibit several faults, the largest of these being the Cliviger Valley Fault. This particular fault runs through the gorge from Todmorden into the Healey Wood district of Burnley. The Fault makes an important contribution to the physical appearance of the valley, as the rocks to the south-west of the fault have been upthrust in relation to the rocks to the north-east. Near Holme Chapel there is a maximum displacement of 1300 feet with the Lower Coal Measures (on the north-east) faulted against the Millstone Grit Series. This has produced the fault line escarpment of Thieveley Scout with its striking crags. In contrast the softer coal measures on the downthrown side of the fault produced relatively gentle relief features.

Over the last million years Britain has been subjected to ice ages when considerable parts of the land surface have been covered by ice sheets. Stones and rocks contained in the base of a glacier acted in an abrasive manner on the land beneath, producing a mass of finely ground 'rock flour'. The melting of the glacier caused the deposition of glaciàl drift, a 'till' (or boulder clay) composed of rock flour, together with any rocks which had been carried along either in the ice or on the surface. In the local area till occurs as a layer of yellow pebbly clay beneath a relatively shallow top soil.

The view from Holme Tunnel top looking towards Copy Pit (E. Fenton). The over-deepened valley contrasts sharply with the relatively flat moorland through which it was carved by glacial water.

Evidence of shallow water deposition of sedimentary rocks.

Quartz pebbles in gritstone, Gorple.

The upper waterfall, Ratten Clough.

False bedding, Beacon Rock. The true beds run horizontally across the photograph.

Ripple marks from Sweet Clough, Lowerhouse.
(Habergham H.S. Collection.)

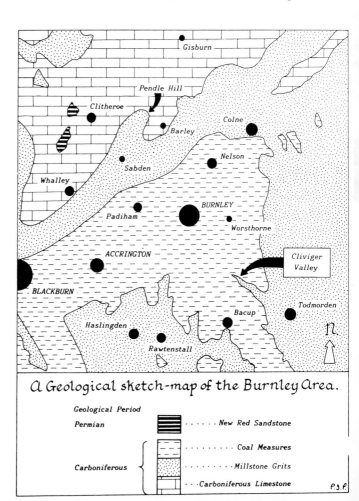

A Geological sketch-map of the Burnley Area.

Gisburn

Pendle Hill

Clitheroe

Colne

Barley

Nelson

Sabden

Whalley

BURNLEY

Padiham

Worsthorne

ACCRINGTON

Cliviger Valley

BLACKBURN

Todmorden

Bacup

Haslingden

Rawtenstall

n

Geological Period		
Permian		· · · · · New Red Sandstone
		· · · · · Coal Measures
Carboniferous		· · · · · Millstone Grits
		· · Carboniferous Limestone

P.S.P.

The conditions leading to the formation of glacial overflow channels. It is understood that some of these channels may actually have been cut beneath the ice sheet.

Lancashire was affected by at least two periods of glaciation which is reflected in the occurrence of two separate tills – the upper and lower deposits. The laying down of the tills was interrupted by an interglacial period when the ice melted due to a milder climate. This period saw the deposition of the sands, silts and gravels which occur between the upper and lower tills.

The height of till deposits on the local hills suggests that prior to the interglacial period the ice sheet covered the land up to a height of 1200 feet. This indicates that ice some 900 feet thick covered the land where Burnley town centre now stands. The Cliviger Valley accommodated an ice flow which probably moved south eastwards.

In the warmer conditions of the interglacial period the ice sheet, which had blocked the Irish Sea and covered much of Lancashire, began to retreat gradually north-westwards. The Pennine moorlands became free of ice before the Whalley area, which meant that the glacial meltwater could not flow via the natural drainage routes to the Irish Sea. Consequently the Cliviger Valley and the hills to the north provide excellent examples of physical features associated with the retreat of glaciation.

Valleys on the western slopes of the Pennine moors were blocked by the edge of the ice sheet, resulting in lakes forming behind the ice 'dams'. The lakes often overflowed across the intervening ridge into the next valley and eroded clearly marked overflow channels which were left high and dry as the ice margin retreated lower down the valleys. Several examples can be seen locally, cutting across the ridges which separate valleys such as Catlow, Thursden, Swinden, Hurstwood and Cliviger. The switchback nature of the Long Causeway results from the road encountering a succession of these channels (at Cartridge Clough, Causeway House, Robin Cross and Mereclough). As the ice margin retreated each channel was abandoned and was replaced by channels at progressively lower levels, the final and lowest being the Mereclough channel.

Water from the Long Causeway channels flowed into the Cliviger Valley which, with the continued retreat of the ice sheet, became a major Pennine overflow channel. The billions of gallons of meltwater pulsing through the Valley were responsible for an overdeepening effect and resulted in the striking gorge which exists today.

In addition to the important part which the melting glaciers played in the shaping of the Cliviger Valley, they left a legacy which helped to determine the land use pattern of the district. The deposition of a sheet of glacial drift throughout East Lancashire produced a heavy, clay soil which restricted the growth of crops. Together with Cliviger's "sloping acres", this resulted in a concentration on stock rearing. Generally the moorlands and steeper slopes are grazed by sheep, and in the lower and gentler parts of the valley dairy cattle are raised.

Glacial overflow channel, The Long Causeway.

The local rocks supported a considerable amount of mining and quarrying. Numerous old coal workings are scattered throughout Cliviger. The first reference to mining in the locality mentions coal extracted from the outcrop of the Arley Seam, close to Riddle Scout, at the beginning of the fourteenth century. Another early pit was in use in the middle of the seventeenth century. According to a report on the Towneley estates, William and Sarah Cockroft were leased a coal mine in the district. The Cliviger Cole and Coke Co. had three pits in the Valley – Union, Walk Mill and Copy. The coal which they mined from the Arley Seam was the best quality for household use. The last few reserves of the Arley coal are still being taken from a private mine near the Long Causeway.

Over six hundred years ago ironstone was mined from workings driven into the north-eastern side of the Valley, opposite to Ratten Clough. Small deposits of lead ore were also worked in the seventeenth and eighteenth centuries. The attempts proved to be unsuccessful and on each occasion the mines were abandoned after a few years.

Mudstones and shales are major sources of brick clays. The Deerplay Quarry was worked by the Enfield Brick and Terra Cotta Co. who produced some of the famous "Accrington Bricks" on the site. Other clays have proved useful economically in the past. The Towneley Coal and Fireclay Co. had workings close to Ratten Clough. Clay extracted from here proved to be very suitable for the baking of fireproof bricks. The Cliviger potters of the last century utilised locally obtained supplies of clay.

Sandstones and flagstones were important sources for building stone, roofing slabs (grey slates) and rubble. The sites of disused quarries exist throughout the Valley and show that both the Coal Measures and the Millstone Grit Series were quarried.

Glacial drift often contains "erratics", rocks which have been transported from their sources by a glacier. The erratics may differ widely from the rocks in the area where they were set down when the ice melted. Locally two types of drift occur. North Western Drift contains erratics from the Lake District and southern Scotland. Limestone erratics are common in the Ribblesdale Drift and the profusion of these rocks in the Shedden Valley supported an ancient lime industry. Limestone pebbles were washed from the glacial drift by "hushing", a process involving the diversion of streams. There are remains of dams, channels and many former lime kilns in the vicinity.

ACKNOWLEDGEMENTS

We are grateful for the help and advice of the following:

The Lancashire County Records Office, for permission to use relevant parts of Greenwoods Map of 1818 and the Ordnance Survey 6" Map of 1848.

Mr. R. Pickles, F.L.A. and Miss Jean Siddall at Burnley Central Library, for period photographs and access to other information.

Mr. E.B. Ashworth, B.A. for reading the script.

Mr. H.R. Rigg and the staff of Towneley Hall for access to materials and information.

Mr. B. Curzon, Towneley Hall Art Gallery and Museum, for permission to view examples of Cliviger pottery.

Mr. W. Macken for information concerning the Odd Fellows.

The Rev. L.W. Savage for permission to view St. John's Church, Holme Chapel.

Mr. B.W. Jeffrey for help with geological photographs.

The Staff of the Curriculum Development Centre, Burnley.

We are grateful to the following residents who have generously given of their time to provide advice and information, and for the loan of documents and old photographs.

Mrs. Georgina Bentley	Mrs. Ruth Moore
Mr. Tom Chapman	Mrs. Ethel Nowell
Miss H. Collinge	The late Mr. Frank Redman
Mr. Edward Fenton	Mr. Alan Scholes
Mr. Eric Halsall	Mr. Jack Simpson
Mr. Eric Halstead	Mr. Clarence Slater
Mrs. Freda Jackson	Mr. Harold Smith
Mr. Fred Little	Mr. J. Titus Thornber, B.Sc.

The two maps in the section devoted to the geology of the district are based on I.A. Williamson's maps in "A Guide to the Geology of the Cliviger Valley" and "The Natural History of the Burnley Area".

All O'er t' Parish.
A First Stroll Around Cliviger.
Errata and Addenda.

P.31 line 4. "Knobstick Row" was
pulled down in the early 1960s.

P.35 Line 8. "The Delph". The name
Middup Quarry appears on an O.S.
six inch map.

Key to map on facing page

Names in italics denote former sites. Exisiting building are shown in
normal types.

1. Fair View.
2. Village Hall.
3. Queens Hotel.
4. Ram Inn.
5. Subway.
6. Berrils Green.
7. Pot Oven.
8. Light Birks.
9. *Steen Delph.*
10. *Pottery Factory.*
11. *Copy Pit.*
12. *Ironstone Mine.*
13. *Fish Pond.*
14. Holme Tunnel.
15. *Thieveley Farm.*
16. Beacon Rock.
17. *Black Clough Colliery.*
18. *Holme Station.*
19. Jumb Hole.

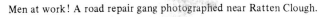

Men at work! A road repair gang photographed near Ratten Clough.